Original title:
42 and Other Answers

Copyright © 2025 Creative Arts Management OÜ
All rights reserved.

Author: Sophia Kingsley
ISBN HARDBACK: 978-1-80566-002-6
ISBN PAPERBACK: 978-1-80566-297-6

The Space Between Questions

In the void where thoughts collide,
Minds adrift, nowhere to hide.
As queries bounce like rubber balls,
We'll laugh at life's confusing walls.

Why's the sky so very blue?
Why's a cat like a shoe?
In riddles lost, we chase the light,
While answers play a game of slight.

When Curiosity Knocks

Beneath the door, a whisper lingers,
A gentle tap from curious fingers.
What lies beyond? What's in store?
A world unknown, so much to explore.

With a twist, the knob reveals,
A jumbled mass of silly feels.
Like a sock, where could it be?
A puzzle wrapped in mystery.

Glimpses of the Unexplainable

In the forest of odd ideas,
Where logic fades and laughter cheers.
We find a duck that quacks a tune,
And moonbeams dancing on a dune.

What's that glow? A jellyfish?
Or just a dream, an oddball wish?
Caught in the web of things unplanned,
We giggle as we try to understand.

Navigating the Abyss of Doubt

Down the rabbit hole we plunge,
With thoughts so wild, they bubble, lunge.
Wading through doubt's murky stream,
We chase the echoes of a dream.

Is gravity more than a mere chance?
Or is belief just a silly dance?
In this chaos, let us play,
For laughter leads the way each day.

Revelations in the Silence

In silence thoughts can bubble,
A number dances, oh so subtle.
Questions rise, like morning dew,
Answers giggle, just for you.

Whispers linger in the air,
Math and jokes make quite a pair.
Add a laugh, subtract your frown,
Witty wisdom wears a crown.

The Labyrinth of Thought

In the maze where ideas play,
Count the signs along the way.
A twist, a turn, a silly plight,
Lost in numbers, found in light.

What can rhyme with every sum?
Count your giggles, here they come!
Step by step, through mental fun,
A riddle waits, and then you run!

The Search for Hidden Meaning

Peeking under every stone,
Searching jokes that stand alone.
In each shadow, laughter hides,
Follow where the humor guides.

Meaning's buried soft and deep,
In quirky dreams, no need for sleep.
Twist it, turn it, do a dance,
Every thought deserves a chance!

Numerology of Existence

In numbers, secrets often lay,
Count your ducks, but which way?
Chase the digits, light and free,
Smiles abound in math's decree.

Life's a puzzle, mixed and fun,
What's the score? We won, we won!
Balance equations with a grin,
In this game, we all must win!

Finding the Unfindable

In a quest for the great unknown,
I stumbled on a gnome with a phone.
He said, "Look not at the stars so vast,
The answer's in your sandwich, thanks to the past."

I asked him, "Is that really true?"
He laughed and said, "Just chew and strew!"
So I munched, and to my delight,
I found the answer wasn't quite right.

Reflections on the Edge of Knowing

I peered into the mirror's face,
For wisdom found in every place.
But all I saw were toothpaste stains,
Reflecting my absurd refrains.

"Is there meaning?" I asked with flair,
The mirror winked, as if to share.
Then off it went, no answers gave,
Just showed me how to misbehave.

The Voyage to Epiphany

I took a boat made out of cheese,
Sailing through thoughts with a gentle breeze.
Fish jumped up to share their views,
Mostly about how to choose the blues.

With sails of crackers, the sunlit glow,
Each wave a riddle, a chance to grow.
But as I drifted, I heard them shout,
"Dear friend, it's all a game, no doubt!"

Simplicity Among Complexity

In tangled webs of thought so grand,
I found a pair of rubber bands.
They snapped and twanged with such delight,
Announcing chaos, oh what a sight!

With every twist, each knot took flight,
Designs emerged with colors bright.
In a world so mixed, here lies the key:
To laugh and play, and just be free!

Harvested from Dreams

In a field where thoughts do grow,
I pluck the clouds, they put on a show.
Carrots of laughter, potatoes of cheer,
The harvest is ripe, come gather near.

Fruits of the mind, a curious mix,
Radishes giggle, tomatoes do tricks.
Dig deep for truth, it's buried in jest,
What's planted in fun surely grows best.

The Veiled Truth Beneath Reality

Behind the curtain, things twitch and sway,
Truth wears a disguise, come out to play.
Unravel the riddles, the whispers of fate,
Twists in the plot make logic sedate.

A chicken debates with a wise old toad,
What's right and proper, down this curvy road.
They ponder existence over a pie,
With sprinkles of nonsense, oh my, oh my!

Phantoms of Lost Knowledge

Ghosts of the past, in libraries roam,
Searching for wisdom in each dusty tome.
They chuckle at answers that danced 'round the room,
While scholars still ponder, they glory in gloom.

With each turned page, a new fable spun,
The punchline forgotten, but oh, the fun!
Phantom professors in debates they persist,
Declaring the meaning—if only we missed!

The Lighthouse in the Fog

In a harbor where logic dares not to tread,
A beacon of humor shines bright overhead.
Waves of confusion, they crash and they roll,
While laughter escapes from the depths of the soul.

Signal fires flicker, with jokes on repeat,
Guiding lost sailors on whimsical feet.
Navigating nonsense, through mist they will steer,
For finding the laughter is why they are here.

The Language of the Stars

The cosmos whispers, a cosmic jest,
A giggle of galaxies, in playful quest.
Planets dance in circles, silly and bright,
While comets wear hats in the deep, starry night.

Asteroids chuckle, they're quite the clowns,
While black holes hum tunes, pulling in frowns.
Constellations wink, they're in on the joke,
Stars trade punchlines, like a celestial bloke.

Unlocking the Unknown

In a box full of keys, I've lost my way,
Each one a riddle, come out to play.
Some fit the locks, but make the door squeak,
While others dance wildly, just hide and sneak.

So I ask the shadows, what's the true key?
They laugh and they twirl like it's all 'bout glee.
The answers are silly, they tickle the brain,
Unlocking life's quirks, like a raucous train.

The Puzzle We Call Life

Life's like a puzzle, with pieces all mixed,
Some fit in just right, while others are fixed.
We search high and low for that one perfect bit,
Only to find it was lost in the pit.

Jigsaw of laughter, or maybe it's tears,
We tackle each puzzle as we face our fears.
With each shape and color, the fun will prevail,
Making sense of nonsense, we laugh without fail.

In Pursuit of Clarity

I chase after clarity, it's quite a spree,
Like finding a cat stuck up in a tree.
It teases me gently, with whispers and grins,
Darting away as my quest begins.

I scribble and scribble, my thoughts are a mess,
With questions like bubbles, they fizz and they bless.
Yet in all the chaos, the fun's in the ride,
For clarity dances, a whimsical guide.

Resonance of Untold Stories

In a world of quirky tales,
Lies a number that prevails,
Answers hidden, jokes on reach,
Wisdom learned, yet out of speech.

A spherical cat does prance,
In shadows of a wild dance,
Counting sheep on clouds so high,
With giggles that can touch the sky.

Knock, knock jokes in cosmic halls,
Echoing through galaxy walls,
Strange horizons, laughter's crest,
Finding joy in every quest.

Flip a coin, make a wish,
In this soup, there's quite a dish,
With each slurp, a twist appears,
Cracking codes of laughing fears.

Between Certainty and Uncertainty

In a dance of what we know,
Where the wild ideas flow,
Certainty takes a silly slip,
As we ride this cosmic trip.

Like a fish that climbs a tree,
Questions loom like a bumblebee,
Buzzing round and round the truth,
With punches packed in jester's tooth.

Logic wears a clownish hat,
While wisdom ponders where it's at,
In the circus of the mind,
Jester's antics left behind.

Mismatched socks and silly shoes,
In life's game, we often lose,
Yet the laughter builds our sky,
As we ponder, ask, and try.

The Colors of Hidden Wisdom

In a palette bright and bold,
Lies a mystery to behold,
Silly shades of what we seek,
Jumbled answers, blissfully weak.

With crayons sprawled across the floor,
We sketch the questions we adore,
A riddle wrapped in candy floss,
Every color comes with gloss.

Wisdom speaks in riddles vague,
While we ponder every stage,
In jest, we peel back the layers,
Finding laughter in the players.

Like a rainbow after rain,
Chasing giggles, never bane,
For in each hue, a truth will sprout,
The joy of knowing what it's about.

Patterns Beneath the Surface

Beneath the waves of what we see,
Lie patterns of curiosity,
Dancing through the unknown night,
Juggling puzzles, pure delight.

A pointed hat and silly broom,
Mysteries brew like springtime bloom,
What once was lost begins again,
In the laughter of old friends.

Hidden codes on coffee cups,
In every swirl, a giggle erupts,
The universe in every sip,
Witty whispers on the trip.

So let's embrace the joyous chase,
In quirky thoughts, we find our space,
As patterns twirl and twist away,
Finding laughter in today.

Discoveries in the Dark

In the shadows, secrets creep,
Whispers giggle while others sleep.
With a flashlight, I take a peek,
Finding truths that seem so bleak.

Socks are never the matched pair,
They haunt my closet, I swear!
Books with covers missing, bare,
In the darkness, what is fair?

A cat with a puzzled face,
Staring at the empty space.
Where did I leave that lost grace?
Perhaps it's gone without a trace.

Mysteries swirl like soap in air,
As I dance on a foolish dare.
Laughing loudly, without a care,
In the dark, joy is everywhere!

Threads of Connection in Silence

In a chat, the words can flip,
Like a fish, they jump and slip.
Silence hangs without a tip,
Yet laughter's just a tiny sip.

Emails sent, then lost in time,
Echoes bounce in perfect rhyme.
Why does my inbox feel like a crime?
Perhaps it's just the postman's mime.

A wink exchanged on crowded bus,
No one sees, it's just for us.
Each glance a secret, in a fuss,
Silly moments all discuss.

With nods and smiles, we weave a thread,
In the quiet, where all is said.
Now my thoughts, they dance and spread,
In silence, humor's sweetly fed!

Journeys of Fractured Reason

I set sail on waves of doubt,
With a compass that spins about.
Each answer leads to another pout,
In the maze, I scream and shout.

Maps of logic turn to clay,
Every path leads me astray.
Why walk straight when I can play?
A crooked smile lights my way.

Cracks in my so-called bright thought,
Each attempt leaves me distraught.
Logic's battles are badly fought,
In the end, it's joy I sought.

With a jigsaw of mismatched truth,
I find wisdom in my youth.
A puzzle where I find my proof,
Fractured pieces dance in sooth!

Unraveling the Tapestry of Thought

Threads hang loose in colors bright,
Weaving tales that spark delight.
Each twist and turn feels just right,
In the tapestry, ghosts take flight.

Ideas tangle like shoelaces,
Chasing whimsy in hidden places.
Every thought's a moonlit face,
In the chaos, joy embraces.

One stitch pulls and starts to fray,
Thoughts can sometimes go astray.
Yet laughter weaves a brighter way,
In this fabric, I choose to play.

As I unravel, surprises bloom,
In the mess, there's always room.
With laughter, I can face the gloom,
Tapestries dance, dispelling doom!

The Answer That Wasn't

I searched for the key, oh what a quest,
In realms of nonsense, I put it to the test.
With riddles and jokes, no wisdom to glean,
Each solution I sought was rarely seen.

A penguin in a top hat, so grand and quite dapper,
Spoke riddles of life, but left me in laughter.
I asked for a secret, a guide, or a clue,
But tickled my brain, then bid me adieu.

One wonder I found, a cat on a swing,
Told tales of great laughter, oh what joy it would bring.
But when I sought answers, it just purred with glee,
A punchline I missed, right under the tree.

So here I remain, with questions in tow,
In the land of the silly, where answers don't grow.
I've learned that the journey is often the treat,
In a world of absurdity, life's whims can't be beat.

In the Shadows of Questions

In corners of thought, where mysteries creep,
Questions arise like the cats that don't sleep.
They hide in the shadows, with giggles and sly,
While answers play hide and seek, oh my!

A mouse with a monocle leads them astray,
Squeaks out the riddles in a whimsical way.
"To find what you seek, you may need a shoe,
Dancing with owls, that's the clue that's for you!"

Around every corner, a giggle lives there,
Wit in disguise, with a wild, crazy flair.
I stumbled upon thoughts that looped in a swirl,
With shadows that chuckled, in a jumbled twirl.

So here in the dark, where the questions play nice,
In the company of dreams, where wonders entice.
I'll dance with my doubts, let my laughter ignite,
In the shadows of whims, everything feels right.

The Dance of Infinite Curiosities

Oh, join in the jig of perplexing delight,
Where questions are partners, dancing in flight.
With leaps into laughter, we spin round and round,
In the hall of the curious, odd truths can be found.

A jester in sneakers, he plays a fine tune,
With melodies bursting like bubbles at noon.
"Why is the sky blue?" they all start to prance,
"Let's spin to an answer, give it a chance!"

Our feet move in rhythm, to riddles we sway,
With puzzles aplenty, we jump and we play.
A kaleidoscope laughter, a whirlwind of fun,
In the dance of the questions, we're all just as one.

So let's twirl with the uncertainties, wildly and free,
In the garden of quirks, where we can just be.
With smiles that linger, we'll cherish this night,
In the dance of infinity, everything feels bright.

Puzzles of the Starry Night

The stars in the sky throw a curious gleam,
Questions like comets, burst forth from a dream.
"What's hiding up there?" I whisper to space,
The cosmos just winks, with a grin on its face.

A riddle unfolds like a blanket of light,
Shooting stars giggle, a charming sight.
"Each answer you seek is a spark in the void,
With laughter and mischief, we'll never be bored."

In this puzzle of wonder, the night starts to twirl,
As mysteries dangle, like jewels that unfurl.
With the moon as my partner, we jest and we play,
In the cosmic ballet, where questions hold sway.

So twinkle and sparkle, dear stars up above,
In this riddle of life, let's laugh and let love.
For the puzzles we ponder are merely a show,
In the starry night's arms, we'll dance to and fro.

Hidden Logic in Plain Sight

In a world where ducks wear ties,
Questions multiply like fruit flies.
How many socks for a tango spin?
Answers hide where antics begin.

Rabbits hop through quantum doors,
As llamas dance on marble floors.
The clock ticks backward, just for laughs,
While squirrels argue with their halves.

Cacti plot in desert heat,
Chasing dreams on little feet.
Lizards gossip in the trees,
Spilling tea with bumblebees.

So chuckle loud, let logic bend,
In silly realms, we all pretend.
For life's a riddle wrapped in jest,
With joy and quirk, we are all blessed.

Refracting Reality Through Time

Time travelers argue with their hats,
Hopping past the teasing cats.
Every second bends with glee,
Wormholes weave through cups of tea.

A calendar's confused delight,
Marks Wednesdays twice, oh what a sight!
While dragons fly through Tuesday's haze,
Chasing clocks in playful ways.

Two stooges claim the cosmic prize,
With jellybeans for alibis.
They float on clouds, in silly bows,
And check their watches filled with prose.

So take a trip beyond the norm,
Where giggles and goofiness swarm.
In this world of time's big trick,
Every punchline comes out thick.

The Unfurling Scroll of Existence

In the library of cosmic fate,
Doodles dance and stylus skate.
Books flip open, laugh and tease,
Pages rustle like a breeze.

Philosophers toast with fizzy drinks,
While cats on shelves roll and wink.
Existence scribbles in pastel ink,
As thoughts collide, and spirits sink.

The wisdom scrolls, wild and free,
Whispering secrets to cats in trees.
Each quip a riddle, each joke a clue,
In the grand banquet for me and you.

So roll the scroll and let it spin,
For life is where the fun begins.
With teacups raised to the absurd,
In every sigh, a chuckle heard.

Patterns in Cosmic Chaos

Stars wear hats made from marshmallows,
Giggles echo from distant shallows.
In spirals of chaos, laughter reigns,
With comets playing silly games.

The universe throws a rolling dice,
With every outcome tasting nice.
Galaxies laugh in cosmic jests,
Plotting chaos on their quests.

Penguins waltz on Saturn's rings,
Juggling dreams and silly things.
The fabric of space, a tapestry,
Weaving quirks for you and me.

So let's embrace this fickle dance,
Where logic lost its second chance.
In patterns of chaos we will find,
A funny tune, or just unwind.

Constellations of Thought

In the sky where ideas float,
Thoughts collide like a grand old boat.
Stars are questions in silly flight,
Chasing answers that dance in light.

Glimmers of wisdom peek and hide,
With cosmic jokes we can't abide.
A quasar giggles, a comet grins,
As we ponder where logic begins.

Wormholes swirl with laughter and glee,
Riddles tickle like a cup of tea.
Each twinkle brings a new surprise,
In the vast unknown, the fun never dies.

So chart your course through wobbly space,
Join the parade of the thinking race.
In the universe's playful scheme,
Let absurdity reign supreme in your dream.

The Mystery of Missing Links

Once upon a time, they said,
A link went lost, or so we dread.
Connecting dots in a silly way,
Turns out it's just on holiday.

Searching high and digging low,
Where would a curious brain go?
Behind the sofa, in the chair,
Missing links are everywhere!

We find a sock, a mystery tale,
Maybe links are on a sail.
Charting waters with jokes in tow,
Navigating laughs wherever we go.

So pat the dog, and drink your tea,
Links might just be a part of me.
In this grand chase, there's no worry,
Just a giggle, don't need to hurry.

Fragments of Infinite Possibilities

In a box of quirky bits and bobs,
Lie slivers of thoughts, like tiny mobs.
Each piece a puzzle that's wildly spun,
Crafting laughter before it's done.

What if cats could fly in style?
Or frogs wore suits and danced a mile?
In a world of whimsies, all can blend,
The funny paths that twist and bend.

Like wisps of smoke on a windy day,
They frolic and ripple, come out to play.
Balloons with faces float in the air,
Every possibility a joke to share.

So weave the threads of joy with care,
In every fragment, life's laughter's rare.
An endless stream of chuckles and cheer,
In the tapestry of thoughts we hold dear.

When Questions Have No End

Why does pizza love a pie?
And how does a balloon kiss the sky?
Questions tumble in a zany dance,
Tripping over answers that romanced.

What makes a shadow giggle at night?
Or why do squirrels enjoy a fright?
Each query spins another round,
In the endless loop of humor found.

Twirling through the comedic haze,
Life's riddles serve laughter's gaze.
With every ponder, a chuckle grows,
In the garden of wit where absurdity flows.

So raise a glass to the curious mind,
The questions that leave us joyfully blind.
In a world where smiles endlessly bend,
Embrace the fun when there's no end.

Mysteries in Numerals

In a world of digits, what do they mean?
We ponder and scratch, with a laugh that's unseen.
Calculators buzzing like bees in a hive,
Chasing the answers that keep us alive.

Riddles in numbers, oh what a delight!
The sum of our laughter is quite out of sight.
Chasing the secrets in every odd sum,
While giggles erupt in a numerical drum.

Think of the puzzles that numbers can weave,
In a sea of confusion, we'll never believe.
Eights look like snowmen, or so we declare,
While sixes and nines dance in whimsical air.

So let's raise a toast, with pi in our glass,
To the math that confounds, yet makes moments pass.
In the chaos of symbols, let joy take the lead,
For laughter in digits is all that we need.

The Silent Solution

In twilight of numbers, answers can hide,
With whispers of math, we take them in stride.
Counting our chuckles, and tossing a coin,
Searching for truths that we can't quite join.

Formulas tangled like spaghetti on plates,
A silent solution, oh, say it relates!
Each gesture a clue, like a dance that we see,
A waltz with the questions, so wild and carefree.

The graph looks perplexing, yet bears a big smile,
Knots in equations that stretch for a mile.
With every few fractions, we giggle and boast,
While pondering deeply, and raising a toast.

So laugh with the numbers, let logic set sail,
In the land of conjectures, we'll never grow stale.
With humor abundant, we'll forge our own way,
In the arithmetic circus, let's dance and play.

Echoes of Curiosity

A riddle or two, like sound waves they swell,
Curiosity tickles, can you hear that bell?
The sound of confusion rings out in the night,
Echoes of laughter that sparkle so bright.

Questions arise like balloons in the sky,
For answers elusive, like fish that swim by.
With each little quirk, we giggle and muse,
In the puzzle of numbers, there's nothing to lose.

What's hidden in symbols, can never be seen,
Like cats in a hat, they're both silly and keen.
Are fractions just fractions, or tales with a twist?
In the echo of queries, do you get the gist?

Join the quest for the quirky, with humor a friend,
In the world of the numbers, the fun never ends.
So let's chase the whispers, the giggles that roam,
In the echoes of curiosity, we'll always feel home.

Beyond the Questions

Out past the queries, where answers reside,
A jolly jaunt through the numbers, let's ride!
With each question blooming like flowers in spring,
Amidst all the laughter that counting can bring.

Each digit a character in this grand play,
Strutting on stages, they dance and they sway.
From one through ten, let's make an arcade,
Where fun is the game, and the odds are mislaid.

The mysteries hidden, like socks in the wash,
Fling them together, go ahead, make a slosh!
With giggles in tandem, we'll solve and we'll cheer,
For beyond all the questions, the answer is clear.

So here's to the numbers, let's crack open cheer,
In the land where we question, let laughter draw near.
For the fun lies in seeking, in jest we shall play,
Beyond all the questions, we'll brighten the day.

Threads of Infinity Weaved

In a loom where questions twine,
A needle of jest, a sip of wine.
Each thread a thought, a curious loop,
Knots that tangle in a cosmic group.

We gather the riddles, unspool the skies,
In a tapestry spun from our why's.
Laughter echoes through the fabric vast,
With every flicker, a question is cast.

So let's thread the seams with our quirkiest dreams,
Plant seeds of nonsense, and watch how it beams.
For in every snare, a joke may reside,
A giggle may linger, though logic may hide.

Thus we weave our wonder, in patterns so bright,
Chasing the shadows, embracing the light.
For in the absurd, we discover the fun,
As threads of infinity dance in the sun.

Conversations with the Abyss

I peered into darkness, said, "What's the deal?"
The abyss just chuckled, said, "I feel real!"
We chatted for hours, about nothing and all,
It echoed back thoughts, like a cosmic call.

"Why do we ponder?" I asked with a grin,
The abyss winked back, "It's where I begin!"
From the depths of confusion, wisdom takes flight,
In the void of the silly, we find pure delight.

We tossed out our questions, like socks on the floor,
The abyss just giggled, could handle much more.
"Let's dive together, let nonsense unfold,
In these depths of laughter, stories are told!"

So we danced with the shadows, a humorous swirl,
In conversations where chaos begins to unfurl.
And I left feeling lighter, my fears in a zip,
For even the void can share in a quip.

The Uncharted Realm of Thought

In a land where reason takes a day off,
Thoughts run amok, like a puppy in scoff.
Here logic is dizzy, and laughter runs wild,
Where the absurdity flows, like a giddy-eyed child.

Navigating the paths of a giggling maze,
Each corner we turn, there's a silly craze.
With questions that spiral, like leaves in the air,
In this uncharted realm, we lighten our care.

We stumble through theories, trip over a pun,
In this wacky wonderland, we're all a bit fun.
The map is a joke, drawn in crayon and fluff,
Who knew that exploring could be so tough?

But in every confusion, a smile will erupt,
In the heart of the realm, our laughter is stuffed.
So we wander forever, with twinkling delight,
In the uncharted domains where nonsense takes flight.

Ponderings of the Infinite

With a cup of tea and a curious grin,
I pondered the cosmos, where thoughts begin.
The infinite beckoned with its whimsical shout,
"Come dance with the stars, let the pondering sprout!"

The math was a riddle, the physics a jest,
In this grand comedy, we're simply a guest.
I counted the galaxies, lost track of the fun,
When I realized giggles are just as profound.

So I scribbled my thoughts on a napkin of fate,
Where laughter and wonder hold hands on a plate.
Each epiphany painted a vibrant delight,
And the universe winked, in its playful light.

Thus I roam through the depths where the silly is vast,
In pondering moments, I'm freed from the past.
For the infinite's beauty is wrapped up in cheer,
Where the questions are many, and the giggles are near.

Singularities in the Universe

In the void where logic breaks,
Gravity hides, and time awakes.
Where cats may dance in quantum plays,
And socks go missing for all days.

Black holes hum a silent tune,
Spinning dreams on a cosmic swoon.
While aliens giggle in their ships,
Counting stars and doing flips.

Strange particles throw wild parties,
Protons showing off their arties.
Neutrons chat on cosmic docks,
As space becomes a paradox.

But isn't this a riotous game,
To ponder space without a name?
With laughter echoing through the stars,
We shrug, and find our joy is ours.

The Allure of the Unknown

What hides beyond the curtain gray?
Mysterious lands where travelers play.
A place where logic loses its way,
And squirrels talk of the price to pay.

The whispers of secrets fill the air,
As people ponder without a care.
Chasing shadows and leading trails,
To cook up fun in a pot of tales.

With riddles bubbling in the breeze,
And answers hiding just to tease.
The charm of questions left untold,
As mysteries in quirks unfold.

In this delightful, silly dance,
Where whimsy reigns and wonders prance,
We giggle at the strange terrain,
Finding joy in the joyful pain.

Unearthing the Ordinary

In the corners where dust bunnies dwell,
We search for treasures—can you tell?
A missing shoe, a half-eaten pie,
A long-lost rubber duck that can fly.

The mundane holds the grandest lore,
A teabag's saga, or a locked door.
With laughter echoing in our hearts,
We find grand tales in tiny parts.

Every spilled drink, a splash of fate,
Turns a mishap into something great.
Ordinary lives, with quirks to spare,
Become a comedy, a breath of air.

So let's dig deep in our cluttered space,
Finding wonders in each little place.
The ordinary shines with a special gleam,
Just look around, and you'll find the dream.

Finding Clarity in the Chaos

Among the jumbled thoughts and rants,
Life's riddles dance like silly ants.
When socks are scattered and time is sparse,
We chase our dreams like a runaway horse.

Maps can twist, and paths may bend,
But confusion makes us laugh and send.
A tumble here, a fumble there,
We rise again with a joyful flare.

Order comes in the oddest ways,
From cereal boxes in wild arrays.
The beauty of moments, mismatched and bright,
Sparks laughter in the soft twilight.

So embrace the mess for what it shows,
The funny side of life's crazy flows.
We find our truth in the lovely grime,
A joyful chaos, a dance with time.

Whispers of the Universe

In cosmic jokes the planets spin,
Stars giggle softly, where to begin?
Galaxies wink and black holes tease,
In the vastness, we float with ease.

Time tickles us in odd ways,
Like a cat with yarn, it plays.
We chase moments, but they flee,
Laughing at our clumsiness, you see.

Einstein chuckles from afar,
While Schrödinger waits, a hidden star.
Quarks dance in a quantum whirl,
Making us question the great big swirl.

We spin in circles, round and round,
Searching for meaning that can't be found.
But isn't it grand, a joyful spree,
In the whispers of the universe, wild and free?

When Numbers Speak

Count the giggles, one, two, three,
Mathematics laughing, can't you see?
Numbers chat with a playful tone,
Multiplying fun in a world of their own.

Pi rolls around, a never-ending tale,
While fractions argue, they just can't prevail.
Algebra's moody, wearing a frown,
But geometry's spinning, swirling around.

Percentages party with cheerful flair,
Dividing the cake, with room to spare.
Statistics giggle at the odds they make,
While calculators fizzle, just can't take a break.

In the world of math, laughter is key,
With every equation, the fun is set free.
So let's dance with numbers, they've got the beat,
In this joyous realm, life feels sweet!

The Search for Meaning

A philosopher stumbles upon a clue,
Chasing shadows, not a clue in view.
He trips on thoughts, lands with a thud,
In the puddles of wisdom, thick as mud.

Questions float like bubbles in air,
Some pop with laughter, others with despair.
The quest for answers, a comical thrill,
Each turn reveals yet another quill.

Maps of existence, doodled in haste,
Drawn with crayons, no time to waste.
Underneath the jest, seekers find gold,
In the funny stories, wisdom unfolds.

So what's the meaning, oh where could it be?
Dancing with laughter, come join the spree.
In the absurd tales, we'll find our way,
In the search for meaning, let's laugh and play!

Threads of Infinity

Spools of yarn unravel in space,
Infinite patterns, a timeless lace.
Weaves of laughter, knots of delight,
Stitching together the day and night.

Tangled thoughts float like clouds,
As wisdom hides beneath the crowds.
In the tapestry, each thread tells a joke,
Intertwining laughter, and a brogued poke.

Infinity giggles, a cosmic seam,
Stitching realities, it's all a dream.
The more we seek, the less we know,
Yet each silly thread continues to flow.

So here we are, in this colorful spin,
Celebrating life's tapestry, our curious kin.
With each knot tied, and each whim shared,
In the threads of infinity, we've all fared!

The Enigma of Life's Code

In a land where questions roam,
Numbers jive and dance like foam.
The answers hide in silly shoes,
Each twist and turn, a baffling muse.

Jesters laugh at puzzles tossed,
With every clue, you wonder what's lost.
The riddles churn like frothy stew,
While squirrels plot to steal your shoe.

Math winks slyly from its cage,
Numbers play like kids on stage.
You crunch and munch on wobbly facts,
Life giggles softly as it distracts.

What's the key? A blank expanse?
Perhaps it's just an awkward dance.
In the chaos, laughter's the prize,
Seek joy in nonsense, oh how it flies!

Insights from the Void

Out in space where stars abound,
Aliens sing in silly sound.
They whisper secrets, oh so sly,
Telling jokes as comets fly.

Bubbles of wisdom float on by,
Like popcorn popping in the sky.
With every blink and cosmic grin,
They ponder life's great riddle spin.

A black hole opens, full of jest,
You might just find a cosmic quest.
They'll ask you questions, twist and shout,
Leaving you laughing, filled with doubt.

What's the truth? A cosmic laugh!
Perhaps the light is just a gaffe.
In the void, humor reigns supreme,
And life's just one big funny dream!

A Journey Through the Unknown

Packing bags full of oddities,
Bound for lands of peculiarities.
Maps are scribbles, directions askew,
Adventure calls from the foggy blue.

Along the path, a talking cactus,
Offers riddles, trades you for practice.
You dodge the trouble, step on toes,
While giggles bubble, oh how it grows!

Trees are dancing, the rocks compose,
Every shadow a comedy shows.
The roads twist like a gummy worm,
As questions sprout in zany form.

What's the end? Just more compile,
Life's a ride, come enjoy the dial.
With laughter echoing far and near,
Every unknown is less severe!

The Wisdom of Stars Aligned

The cosmos whispers through the night,
Aligning stars, what a sight!
They chuckle softly, share their tales,
Of mischief, laughter, and comet trails.

Celestial jesters, twinkling bright,
Spin the wheel, set dreams alight.
Seek wisdom in their stellar fun,
Life's a game, no need to run.

Asteroids wink, planets play peek,
In this universe, it's joy we seek.
Galaxies swirl in a hilarious plot,
Each cosmic punchline hits the spot.

So when stars align, join their cheer,
Dance with the cosmos, hold life dear.
In the laughter of the night sky's throne,
We find our truth, we're never alone!

The Cosmic Query

In a vast cosmic dance, they twirl and spin,
Trying to find answers, where do we begin?
With questions galore, and no hints in sight,
They trip over stardust, what a silly plight!

Aliens chuckle, sipping space tea,
While humans are lost, searching for glee.
They shuffle through galaxies, heads spinning round,
Hoping a clue in the void can be found.

Secrets of the Infinite

In the realm of the strange, odd secrets reside,
With winks from the cosmos, and giggles inside.
Why do socks disappear? They giggle and pry,
Turns out they joined a parade in the sky!

Counting the stars is a task quite absurd,
Like lost in a maze where no one has heard.
Each twinkle a riddle, with humor galore,
The universe chuckles, who's keeping score?

A Journey Through Paradox

A cat's in a box, meowing with glee,
Is it dead? Is it live? Who's asking, not me!
Socks on the moon have begun to collide,
In the land of the strange, where facts can't abide!

Why does time tick backwards, while forward we go?
We all laugh at the nonsense, what a wild show!
Lost in a loop, hands waving around,
In a quirky reality, where logic is drowned.

The Answer Within the Void

The void is a vast, hollow cosmic joke,
With echoes of laughter each time the stars poke.
Is there sense in the chaos, or just a sly nod?
Where whimsy and wisdom dance on the sod!

As we ponder our fates, twirling in space,
The answers are hidden, in this merry chase.
A wink from the dark, a giggle's reprise,
In the heart of the void, truth's shrouded disguise.

Moments of Profound Awareness

In the depths of my tea cup, I found a clue,
A sock in the dryer, what more could ensue?
The cat on the bookshelf, a sage with a smile,
Sipping on wisdom, I ponder awhile.

Why do we argue with echoes of thought?
Over chocolate cake, ideas are caught.
A pickle that dances, a rubbery gnome,
In moments like these, we're never alone.

Life is a circus, with clowns on parade,
With pie-in-the-face and confetti displayed.
Each blunder a comic, each thought a grand jest,
In profound awareness, we're simply perplexed.

So rise with the sun, let the humor unfold,
In the quirks of existence, let laughter be bold.
With giggles and snickers, let joy take its flight,
In profound awareness, the world feels just right.

The Riddle of Existence

A chicken crossed over, was it for a quest?
Or just for that tasty worm, 'twixt fowl and fest?
With feathers a-fluffing, and a wink from the sky,
The riddle of life, oh my, oh my!

An octopus juggling, in a bright purple suit,
As fish play marbles with laughter to boot.
What's better than wisdom? More snacks, I propose,
In puzzles like these, curiosity grows.

Why do the cars need wheels, I declare?
Do fish enjoy swimming in bubbles of air?
The universe whispers in quirky designs,
With riddles and giggles, the answer aligns.

So chuckle at chaos, let nonsense ensue,
The riddle of life has no one answer, it's true.
For in the peculiar, we find our delight,
In the jest of existence, the world feels so right.

Illuminations of an Open Mind

With toasters that talk and shoes that can dance,
The world spins and twirls, a curious trance.
An open mind wanders, through legends and dreams,
Finding joy in the wackiest of themes.

A squirrel on a skateboard, with cap on his head,
Racing through life, on laughter he's fed.
The universe chuckles, as we trip on our shoes,
In the illuminating chaos, you'll never lose.

What if the moon's made of soft creamy cheese?
Or if time's just a tickle, meant to tease?
With wonder as compass, we stroll down the lane,
In the quest of absurd, we've nothing to feign.

So dance with the shadows, laugh with the sun,
In the light of absurdity, let's all become one.
With an open mind soaring, the skies are so wide,
Illuminations of whimsy, come take a wild ride!

Signals from the Beyond

The toaster's a prophet, it pops with delight,
Messages from breakfast that set the sun bright.
The cat's been appointed, a sage from the stars,
Decoding the secrets from Venus and Mars.

With pancakes as pancakes, and syrup like truth,
We trust the absurd for the wisdom of youth.
A donut in orbit, a muffin Named Fred,
Signals from the beyond, in sweetened bread.

What if the plants can speak fluent dog?
Or if clouds hold meetings beneath a thick fog?
In the giggles of nature, we see strange signs,
Where mysteries linger, a jest now aligns.

So listen to whispers, both silly and wise,
In the laughter of life, find the grand surprise.
For signals from beyond are there, can't you see?
In the dance of existence, we're wild and free!

The Unwritten Solutions

In the land where numbers play,
Riddles dance in bright array.
Whispers of the cosmic joke,
Laughter hides in every poke.

Puzzles tangled, minds anew,
Searching for a funny clue.
What's the secret, can you see?
It's just math's absurdity!

Life's a quiz with wacky turns,
Every blunder, how it churns.
Looking for the perfect rhyme,
Finding joy in silly time.

Chasing crumbs of logic's pie,
Who knew truth could make us sigh?
In guesses wild, we find delight,
As laughter leads us through the night.

Sifting Through Stardust

Amidst the stars, we search for sense,
Like cosmic kids, it's quite intense.
With magic dust upon our shoes,
We dance on questions, never snooze.

Galaxy's jokes blaze bright and loud,
While black holes tease the curious crowd.
Comets with tails of cotton candy,
We chase the weird, the strange, the dandy.

Nebulas sigh with a wink,
Gravity draws us close to think.
What's the answer? Who can tell?
It's a stardust game we know so well.

Through cosmic fun, we spin around,
In the chaos, joy is found.
Let's toss our doubts to the moon,
And laugh like stars, we'll be there soon.

Paradoxes of Perception

What's real and what's a trick?
Time stands still, then moves too quick.
Lies disguised as truth's intent,
Nonsense reigns, it's heaven-sent.

In circles we dance, lost in thought,
Every answer's another knot.
Logic flips, and reason plays,
In the funhouse of wacky ways.

Mirrors showing left as right,
Laughing at the spin of light.
Every paradox brings a grin,
As we tumble, lose, and win.

So here we are, in wobbly glee,
Finding joy in absurdity.
Reality's just a quirky game,
In this wild and funny frame.

The Language of Infinity

In loops and curves, the tales unwind,
Words abound, the riddles bind.
A jester's laugh in endless scrolls,
As logic skips and chaos rolls.

Counting stars with quirky flair,
Every number throws a dare.
What's beyond that cosmic gate?
A punchline lost? A twist of fate?

Poems scribbled on a breeze,
In the void, we find our keys.
A universe of nonsense plays,
Where wisdom wears a funny gaze.

So join the fun, let laughter ring,
In infinite jest, let's dance and sing.
With every turn, we find the light,
In the language of delight tonight.

The Alchemy of Ideas

In a cauldron of thoughts, we mix and stir,
A sprinkle of chaos, a dash of absurd.
Adding in laughter, a pinch of delight,
Creating a potion that glows in the night.

The wizards of wisdom, with hats askew,
Transforming the mundane into something new.
They juggle with meanings, they twist and they bend,
In the alchemy of ideas, there's always a trend.

From puns that dance lightly on tongues that are dry,
To riddles that tickle and make the brain fly.
Each thought is a bubble, each chuckle a spark,
In this playful pursuit, there's never a dark.

So grab your quill, let your imagination run,
We'll concoct some mischief, share joy and have fun.
The world is our canvas, let's riot and cheer,
In the alchemy of ideas, let's draw them near.

Quantum Leaps of Understanding

In a universe swirling, we leap with a grin,
Where logic can falter, and nonsense can win.
We spiral through theories that twist and enthrall,
With quantum confetti, we dance at the ball.

Each question, a particle, jumps and it plays,
Entangled in laughter, it flutters and sways.
In this realm of confusion, we bounce like a ball,
With answers like shadows, giggling through it all.

The time-space continuum shimmers with joy,
Each thought that we fathom, a subatomic toy.
In a blink of an eye, we twist and we twirl,
With jokes that defy every logical whirl.

So bounce off reality, let your mind drift away,
In leaps of the quirky, we'll dance through the day.
With science as our partner, we'll caper and spin,
In the quantum of funny, let the laughter begin.

Veils of Reality

Behind curtains of nonsense, peeking just so,
Reality whispers, 'Come join the show!'
With each veil we lift, a giggle's released,\nThe truth is a jester, to say the least.

Masked in fine fabric, the real seems a jest,
Where clarity wobbles and doesn't know rest.
The wise men in robes offer tips that confound,
With riddles confetti'd and answers unbound.

Through layers of meaning, we chuckle and pry,
Discovering nonsense that soars through the sky.
With each thread unraveled, our laughter ignites,
In the dance of perception, we reach dizzy heights.

So lift up your veil, let's have a good peep,
Awash in the whimsy, we tumble, we leap.
Each moment is playful, a joke to unveil,
In the tapestry woven, we laugh without fail.

Delving Deeper into Shadows

In the depths of the dark where the shadows convene,
We wander like cats, spry, silly, and keen.
With whispers of mischief, they beckon us near,
To delve into secrets, with giggles, we cheer.

Poking at ponderings, that dance in the gloom,
Unraveling mysteries that bubble and bloom.
Each shadow a jester, plays tricks on the mind,
With riddles that baffle, clever and unkind.

We slip through the cracks where the weirdness entwines,
In the depths of the shadows, where playful design shines.
Every corner of darkness, a joke just in wait,
To brighten our journey, it's never too late.

So let us explore where the giggles reside,
In the dimly lit corners, let joy be our guide.
For in delving deeper, we'll find who we are,
Just silly, sweet souls, like a wish on a star.

The Algebra of Existence

In math we trust, the numbers play,
Chasing solutions that run away.
Add a joke, subtract the frown,
Life's a puzzle spun around.

X marks the spot, or so they say,
Divide your cake, let laughter sway.
Equations dance in quirky loops,
Oh, the conundrums of clever troops.

Count your cats, but not your woes,
Shift each variable, see how it goes.
A plus B might equal fun,
In this class, we've almost won!

Mathletes cheer with secret glee,
While pi takes us to infinity.
Though answers come, they often stray,
Let's just laugh and dance the day.

Reflections in the Abyss

Gazing deep, what do I see?
A clumsy fish who's laughing at me.
The mirrors twirl with giggles bright,
Deep in thought, what a silly sight.

When shadows whisper jokes so sly,
Even the echoes wonder why.
In this chasm of uneven glee,
I trip on my thoughts, absurdity.

Waves of wisdom wash in waves,
Bubbles rise, it's laughter's grave!
Splash around in comic pools,
Where silliness breaks all the rules.

From brink to brink, the fun cascades,
In reflections, truth masquerades.
So dive on in, don't be so stiff,
Embrace the jest, take a wild riff!

Deciphering the Enigma

What's the riddle? What's the clue?
A pickle jar's as deep as blue.
Find the answer, peek inside,
Oh wait, it's just a cat that hides.

Puzzles twist and turn about,
With every try, a goofy shout.
Hidden gems in simple sights,
Like socks that vanish in the nights.

Sneaky answers play their game,
Like roast chicken mad at shame.
Is the secret under our nose?
Or simply lost among our toes?

So grab your hat, your sleuthing gear,
Let's crack the case with lots of cheer.
In every quirk, some wisdom's tight,
But mostly, it's a funny fight!

A Dance of Ideals

Two left feet in grand ballet,
Twirl of thoughts that slip away.
Chasing dreams on hopes' soft toes,
Who knew ideals came with woes?

Step to the left, then swing around,
Life's a dance with ups and downs.
With every stumble, laughter's near,
In this absurdity, we cheer!

Partners change, the music's loud,
Waltzing through this silly crowd.
Jumbled wits in pirouette,
Should we giggle or fret a bit?

So sync your feet, don't be a bore,
Life's a stage, that's for sure.
Join the jig, let laughter take lead,
In this dance, we're always freed!

The Riddle of Time

Tick tock, the clock does play,
What's a minute without some sway?
Counting seconds, never sweet,
Chasing moments on my feet.

Hours blend, they twist and bend,
As if they're joking, around the bend.
Time's a prankster, laughs do flow,
Always faster, never slow.

Shadows of Understanding

In the dark, shadows dance and tease,
Making sense of whispers with ease.
A riddle here, a puzzle there,
Who needs answers? It's just a scare!

Glitches in logic, oh what a sight,
Trying to grasp it, but it takes flight.
Logic's a friend, but what a clown,
Always turning thoughts upside down.

Beyond the Binary

On and off, a simple game,
But wait! It's never quite the same.
Zeros laugh, ones roll their eyes,
In a world where logic flies.

Dancing pixels in a grid,
Silly battles, where truth is hid.
Is it light? Is it shade?
What's right or wrong, in this charade?

The Weight of Wonder

Heft of questions, deep as space,
Holding wonder with a grin on its face.
A wink from the universe, how absurd,
Whispering secrets, rarely heard.

With each curiosity, a chuckle grows,
The more we ponder, the stranger it shows.
A lighthearted chase through thought's vast land,
In the end, it's all just grand!

The Answers That Await

In the cupboard of confusion, where socks disappear,
Lie answers wrapped in riddles, oh so near.
They giggle like the wind, whispering loud,
Promises of wisdom that'd impress any crowd.

Jokes tickle the senses, like a cat on a spree,
One question leads to another, like branches of a tree.
A squirrel lost in thought, oh where did he roam?
Searching for the punchline, far from his home.

The clocks all run backward in this curious place,
Time dances like a jester, in a comical race.
Each puzzle a giggle, each query a jest,
The more that I ponder, the less I can rest.

So let's sip some nonsense, and dine on the strange,
For answers in laughter are free to exchange.
In this banquet of banter, we find our delight,
Mixing questions with humor, from morning 'til night.

Beneath a Sky of Questions

Beneath a sky that's chattery, stars spell out clues,
Questions frolic like puppies, bending the rules.
A comet brings chuckles, a moon made of cheese,
Wonders hover around, hoping to please.

A wise old owl chuckles, 'Who? Me? Really?'
With laughs echoing softly, his wisdom is silly.
Where is the end of the rainbow? A question so bright,
Or just a pot of glitter, hiding in plain sight?

Clouds gather for meetings, debating what's real,
As a fish on a bicycle starts to reveal.
Each inquiry like bubbles in a fizzy delight,
Floating upwards with laughter, forgetting the night.

So let's ponder together, beneath playful skies,
For answers are balloons, waiting to rise.
The wind may take them, yet they dance in the air,
Charming us into joy, with questions to share.

The Essence of Inquiry

In the realm of the quirky, where oddities play,
Questions prance around, in a ludicrous way.
Why do ducks quack with such flair and finesse?
Is it all just a show? Who's taking a guess?

The essence of questions, like syrup on toast,
Makes mornings delightful, we ponder the most.
Is the universe ticklish? Will the planets conspire?
Or is it simply a game of cosmic satire?

Silence wears a tutu, and speaks in a hum,
While logic takes a break, hearing riddles that come.
Nonsense flies in circles, giggling through time,
Dancing on tightropes, in rhythm and rhyme.

So ask all your wonders, let perplexity reign,
For laughter is the answer, that never feels plain.
In the theater of thinking, let's chuckle and sway,
For the journey holds secrets, in the oddest of ways.

Harmonies of Certainty

In a garden of questions, truth blossoms like flowers,
Each petal a puzzle, blooming for hours.
A bee buzzes wisdom, sprinkled with cheer,
Sipping from laughter, it makes all things clear.

A symphony of queries fills the air with delight,
Playing notes of confusion, all day and night.
With a wink and a grin, the answers dance free,
To a tune that's as silly as it can be.

Chase the shadows of doubt, like a cat on the run,
For certainty bubbles, in jokes and in fun.
So tune in to laughter, let logic unwind,
In harmonies sweet, the meaning we find.

For in this jolly chaos, we make peace with the strange,
And embrace every question, love the way they arrange.
With smiles as our compass, we journey with glee,
In this whimsical choir, forever carefree.

The Quest for Cosmic Clarity

In a galaxy far, far away,
A squirrel sought wisdom each day.
With nuts in a bag, oh what a sight,
He pondered the stars, both day and night.

The penguin said, "You're barking mad!"
The squirrel replied, "Not a bit sad!"
"For every star shines just for me,
I'll find the truth, just wait and see!"

He tripped on stardust, rolled in space,
Encountered a worm with a silly face.
They shared a laugh, a chicken joke,
The cosmic quest turned 'round with a poke.

But clarity came, oh what a jest,
In chaos and giggles, he found his rest.
The universe chuckled, both wide and deep,
"Just keep it silly, and don't lose your sheep!"

Secrets in the Silence

In quiet corners where echoes hide,
A cat with a secret took a glide.
She purred to the moon, as wise as can be,
"Meow, I'll tell you, if you share with me."

The moon just chuckled, a grin on its face,
"I can't share much, but I love this place!"
"You see those stars, they twinkle so bright,
They're just swimming in soup, all day and night!"

Then came a frog with a leap so grand,
He croaked, "These secrets? They're unplanned!"
With a hop and a skip, he danced around,
"Shhh, keep it quiet, or we'll lose our sound!"

The cat and the moon shared giggles and grins,
In the silence, the laughter begins.
So if you hear whispers that seem a bit odd,
Just know they're secrets from laughter-loving God!

Beyond the Veil of Numbers

In a realm where numbers twist and twirl,
Lived a jester named Math, with a big, funny swirl.
He added some giggles and subtracted a frown,
With division of laughter, he crowned the clown.

He asked the digits, "What's the score?"
They answered his riddle with a loud 'more!'
"But what is more?" he pondered aloud,
A zero replied, "Just join the crowd!"

Infinity laughed and made a large mess,
As fractions danced around in a colorful dress.
"Don't take it so seriously, let's all have fun!"
The jester declared, "We're never done!"

So if you count up to one hundred and two,
Remember the jester and all the crew.
For behind every equation lies a goofy spark,
In the veil of numbers, we find our mark!

Whispers of the Universe

The universe whispered a secret so sly,
To a dog on a planet with stars in the sky.
He wagged his tail, and with a bark,
"What's the scoop, oh cosmic spark?"

"The answer you seek, my furry friend,
Is found in the laughter that doesn't end!"
The stars giggled, a chuckling spree,
As the moon danced in glee, saying, "Just be free!"

The dog spun in circles, a sight so great,
Chasing his tail while pondering fate.
"What's the meaning, oh vast and wide?
Is there a truth I can't just hide?"

The whispers grew louder, a symphony bright,
"Life's absurdity is your biggest delight!
Keep barking at answers and chasing the light,
For laughter's the wisdom that's always in sight!"

Echoes of a Thousand Thoughts

In a world where questions grow,
Answers hide like shy young mice.
We chase them down with laughs and woe,
But find they're not so very nice.

Counting stars or nose hairs too,
What's the meaning? Who can tell?
The more we search, the more we screw,
And yet we giggle, all is swell.

Clocks don't tick, and socks go missing,
Philosophers trip over their pens.
In this maze of thoughts, we're kissing
The charm of silly, where it ends.

So raise a glass to weird ideas,
Toast to questions that go astray.
Life's a riddle, wrapped in cheers,
Let's laugh our way through every day.

The Mystique of Unseen Truths

In the attic of the mind, it seems,
Dusty truths lie in piles high.
Open a box, and hear the screams,
Of facts that run and truths that fly.

A cat can talk, or so it's said,
While squirrels plot world domination.
With each weird thought, we dance and tread,
On ideas born of imagination.

Check the fridge for space-time bends,
A pickle jar with wisdom rare.
Is the light on? The fun never ends,
In this circus of giggles everywhere.

So twist your mind and stretch it wide,
To find the secrets stuck in a jar.
With nonsense dreams, we will abide,
Riding through life on a shooting star.

Serendipity's Equation

What's X times Y in a world upside down?
Is it laughter that makes numbers dance?
When life gives clowns an old, red crown,
    We find joy in the strangest chance.

Two plus two may equal a pie,
If you choose to think with a quirky view.
What's the sum of a laugh and a sigh?
Call it dinner for the bizarre crew!

Stumble on answers like tripping on air,
    Mixed signals lead to a funky tune.
Birds wear hats and don't have a care,
While squirrels recite the moon's high noon.

So crunch the numbers, toss them high,
    In this messy math of kooky delight.
With whimsical logic, none can deny,
We'll solve life's puzzles, tucked in the night.

Tales of the Unsolved

Oh, what a plot of unsolved lore,
From the case of the missing shoe.
Each clue we chase, seeking for more,
Yet find we're left right in the blue.

Gnomes that dance on garden stakes,
Revealing nothing but silly pranks.
Watch out for questions that life makes,
As laughter sneaks in, giving winks and flanks.

The mystery of socks that disappear,
Or why do puppies dig up the ground?
In this comedy of chaos, we cheer,
For every riddle has a silly sound.

So gather 'round for tales anew,
Of oddities that baffle the mind.
With every laugh, we'll find a clue,
In this merry chase where joy's unconfined.

The Secrets of Ocean Depths

Beneath the waves, fish dance and twirl,
A whale's joke sends bubbles in a whirl.
Jellyfish giggle, glowing in the dark,
Coral reefs hide secrets, weird and stark.

An octopus draws with eight-armed flair,
While crabs wear hats – do they really care?
The seaweed sways to a tune of glee,
As starfish throw a party, just wait and see.

Seashells whisper tales of the ocean wide,
Eels tell stories that they can't abide.
Fish in tuxedos strut with style,
While sea turtles grin, "Stay for a while!"

Bubbles pop like laughter all around,
In this deep blue realm, humor knows no bound.
Deep beneath the waves, joy drifts and dips,
As the ocean laughs with painted fish lips.

The Labyrinth of Inquiry

In a maze of questions, round and round,
Lost in thoughts where no one is found.
A riddle giggles, hiding in the twist,
And the answer ducks, like it's missed the bus.

Each corner holds a curious cat,
Pondering why that dog wears a hat.
Maps of nonsense lie on every shelf,
Whispering secrets, "Just ask yourself!"

A door swings open with a creaky laugh,
Leading to nowhere, or maybe a bath?
The walls are listening, their ears all perked,
Awaiting the answers that sometimes get shirked.

With every step, ideas collide,
As squirrels debate if they should hide.
A chalkboard stands, scribbled full of doubt,
While a voice in the shadows scream, "To get out!"

Flights of Imagination

Up in the sky, a llama takes flight,
With googly eyes, it's quite the sight!
Bubble-wrapped clouds float high and wide,
As kites weave stories on the wind's slide.

A penguin in sunglasses slides on by,
Playing frisbee with a crooked pie.
Unicorns giggle, painted bright,
While rainbows tickle with their soft light.

Sailing on dreams, we're human kites,
With cotton candy clouds and starry nights.
Imagination throws its arms up high,
"Come take a ride, you'll learn to fly!"

Everyone joins, what a lively show,
In a world where whimsy is free to flow.
As thoughts take off, no pilot's need,
For laughter is the compass, yes indeed!

Words Unspoken

In silent rooms where whispers play,
Words tumble softly, finding their way.
A dog winks secretively at a cat,
While the goldfish rolls its eye, just like that.

Breezes carry gossip from leaf to leaf,
As trees chuckle softly, "What a belief!"
Unsaid emotions float in the air,
Making funny faces, here and there.

In the blink of a glance, laughter ignites,
As friends share chuckles, scaling new heights.
Socks lost in laundry swap silly tales,
Of epic socks battles and fabric gales.

Between the lines, a story unfolds,
Tales of the quiet, of silence bold.
And every unspoken jest makes its stand,
Filling the void with laughter so grand.

Answers Unseen

In the cupboard of questions, answers abide,
Hiding from seekers who are ready to slide.
A clock ticks backward, jesting with time,
While socks debate the reason for rhyme.

Wit creeps around corners, a playful sprite,
Carving up puzzles late into the night.
Balloons talking nonsense in vibrant plots,
While mice engage in dance-offs with thoughts.

Beneath a pile of books, a giggle stirs,
As riddles bounce like rubbery furs.
Each page a portal to the bizarre,
Where logic lives under the light of a star.

These unseen answers tickle the mind,
In the labyrinth of chatter, surprises you'll find.
With laughter as compass, we wander so free,
Searching for meanings that tease, not decree.

www.ingramcontent.com/pod-product-compliance
Lightning Source LLC
Chambersburg PA
CBHW051658160426
43209CB00004B/948